# ROVANIEMI TRAVEL GUIDE 2023

A Winter Wonderland: A Guide To Rovaniemi And Lapland. An Idyllic Holiday Destination

**NICOLAS MENDEZ**

## All Right Reserved!

No Part of this book may be reproduced, stored in a retrieval system, or transmitted in any form or by any means, electronic or mechanical, photocopying, recording or otherwise, without the prior written permission of the copyright owner

Copyright © Nicolas Mendez, 2023

## Table of Contents

**INTRODUCTION**

**GETTING STARTED: Essential Travel Information for Rovaniemi**

**A QUICK OVERVIEW OF ROVANIEMI: The Land of the Arctic Wonders**

**PREPARING FOR YOUR TRIP: Ensuring a Seamless Arctic Adventure**

**ACCOMMODATION IN ROVANIEMI: Where Arctic Comfort Awaits**

**GETTING AROUND ROVANIEMI: Exploring the Beauty of the Arctic**

**EXPLORING ROVANIEMI: A Journey through Arctic Wonders**

**OUTDOOR ADVENTURES IN ROVANIEMI: Embrace Arctic Thrills**

**EXPERIENCING FINNISH CULTURE: A Gastronomic Journey Through Finnish Cuisine**

**EMBRACING THE FINNISH SAUNA TRADITION**

**& SPA RETREATS: Saunas and Wellness in Finland**

**FESTIVALS AND EVENTS: Celebrating the Spirit of Rovaniemi Year-Round**

**BEYOND ROVANIEMI**

**LAPLAND ADVENTURES: Snowmobiling in the Wilderness**

**PRACTICAL INFORMATION: Rovaniemi's shopping**

**COMMUNICATION AND CONNECTIVITY IN ROVANIEMI**

**ROVANIEMI TRAVEL ADVICE AND RESOURCES: Maximizing Your Arctic Adventure**

**LANGUAGE GLOSSARY: Common Finnish Phrases for Your Trip to Rovaniemi**

**CONCLUSION: Embrace the Arctic Magic of Rovaniemi**

**BONUS: When Visiting Rovaniemi, There Are 14 Things You Should Never Do.**

# INTRODUCTION

Thank you for visiting the "**Rovaniemi Travel Guide 2023.**" Your ticket to an enchanted tour through one of Finland's most alluring locales is this guide. Rovaniemi, which is located in the heart of Lapland, entices visitors with its distinctive fusion of Finnish charm and Arctic splendor.

We cordially welcome you to explore the charm of Rovaniemi in our thorough guide, a city where tradition and modernity dance mesmerizingly together.

You can discover all the information you need to organize your trip on these pages, from useful travel advice to cultural insights. Discover the city's fascinating past, see its breathtaking scenery, and get immersed in Finnish culture. Rovaniemi guarantees an amazing experience, whether you're following the Northern Lights, seeing Santa Claus in his town, or going on exhilarating Arctic expeditions.

Let this guide serve as your dependable travel companion so that your time in Rovaniemi is memorable and full of wonder. Welcome to Rovaniemi, the city where Arctic fantasies come true.

**Welcome to Rovaniemi: Embracing Arctic Enchantment**

Rovaniemi, the capital of Finnish Lapland, is a location that captures the romance and mystery of the Far North since it is tucked away within the Arctic Circle. As soon as you enter this magical city, you'll discover that it effortlessly combines history and contemporary, providing visitors of all types with a unique and enthralling experience. We'll explore what makes Rovaniemi unique and why it's a must-see location in 2023 in this part.

## About Rovaniemi: Where Tradition Meets Innovations

Rovaniemi, located in the center of Lapland, is significant to Finnish history and culture. It is one of the oldest cities in Northern Finland and has strong ties to the indigenous Sami culture. It was founded in 1639.

The city has changed throughout the years, embracing innovation and expansion while conserving its history.

Its closeness to the Arctic Circle is Rovaniemi's most recognizable characteristic. A short drive from the city center will take you over the Arctic Circle. Due to its unique geographic position, Rovaniemi enjoys the captivating Midnight Sun in the summer and is a great place to search for the elusive Northern Lights in the winter.

Rovaniemi's association with Santa Claus is another important component of its character. Santa Claus Village, where guests may encounter the jolly old guy all year long, is located through the Arctic Circle. The spirit of Christmas is always present there.

The University of Lapland and the Arktikum Science Center, which are pioneers in the study of the Arctic environment, culture, and sustainable development, are among the institutions at the center of the city's research and education in the Arctic. The strategic location of Rovaniemi makes it an obvious hub for these activities.

**Why Visit Rovaniemi: A Year-Round Wonderland**
The all-year-round attractiveness of Rovaniemi makes it a top choice for tourists looking for life-changing adventures.

**Winter Wonders**

Rovaniemi provides some of the greatest opportunities to see the captivating Northern Lights. For the best viewing circumstances, pursue this natural phenomenon on guided trips that take you far from the city lights.

**Snow Adventures**: Enjoy exhilarating snowmobile safaris, husky sledding, and reindeer sleigh rides through beautiful, snow-covered landscapes to immerse yourself in the winter wonderland. Visit Santa Claus in his homeland, where the holiday spirit permeates every day, at Santa Claus Village. Send mail from the Arctic Circle while exploring Santa's post office and getting to know his reindeer.

**Summer Delights**

Experience the extraordinary Midnight Sun phenomenon, in which the sun never sets throughout the summer. It's the ideal time for golfing in the golden light, river cruises, and walks beneath the midnight sun.

**Outdoor Adventures:** Take part in outdoor pursuits like hiking, fishing, and kayaking to discover Rovaniemi's luxuriant woods, spotless rivers, and crystal-clear lakes.

**Sami Culture**: Gain knowledge of the native Sami culture and have the chance to interact with Sami people, participate in their customs, and eat traditional Sami food.

**Year-Round Attractions**

**Arctic Wildlife Park**: A short drive from Rovaniemi, the Ranua Wildlife Park offers up-close encounters with Arctic wildlife including polar bears, reindeer, and Arctic foxes.

Discover the history, present, and future of the Arctic with the help of interactive exhibits and displays at the Arktikum Science Center.

Explore Rovaniemi's thriving cultural scene by visiting the art galleries, museums, and theaters that highlight the local talent and history.

**Making the Most of Your Visit by Planning Your Trip**

Now that Rovaniemi has captured your attention, it's time to organize your trip to this arctic wonderland. Following are some crucial pointers to make your vacation smooth and memorable:

1. **Best Time to Visit**

Visit between **November** and **March** to see the Northern Lights and winter activities.

Plan your vacation between **May** and **August** to take advantage of the summer activities and the Midnight Sun.

## 2. Accommodation Options

Luxury hotels with arctic views, modest cottages, and unusual glass igloos for seeing the Northern Lights are all available as lodging options in Rovaniemi.
It's best to make reservations well in advance, particularly during popular times of the year.

## 3. Clothing and Gear

Even in the summer, dress warmly in layers since temperatures might change.
The majority of tour companies provide the necessary clothes and equipment for winter sports.

## 4. Northern Lights Tours

For the finest opportunities to see this spectacular natural display, join a guided Northern Lights trip. Guides can assist with photography and know where to get the best views.

## 5. **Santa Claus Village**

To accommodate for any unforeseen delays, schedule your visit to Santa Claus Village early in your journey.
Send a postcard with an Arctic Circle postmark, please.

## 6. **Local Cuisine**

Try classic Finnish fare including salmon soup, Karelian pastries, and reindeer stew.
Try regional specialties like Sámi food and cloudberries at real eateries.

## 7. **Communication and Language**

The official languages are Finnish and Swedish, however, English is also commonly used.
For convenience, have a phrasebook or translation software with you.

## 8. **Health and Safety**

Finland is renowned for being secure. But use caution and heed safety advice from guides while engaging in outdoor activities.
Make sure your travel insurance includes medical emergency coverage.

**Finally**, Rovaniemi appeals as a city where the magic of the Arctic meets cultural tradition. Rovaniemi offers a voyage full of surprise and discovery, whether you're looking for the exhilaration of snowy adventures, the mystery of Santa Claus, or the beauty of the Midnight Sun.

# GETTING STARTED: Essential Travel Information for Rovaniemi

To guarantee a smooth and comfortable trip, it is important to provide yourself with the necessary travel knowledge before setting off on your vacation to Rovaniemi. Before visiting this magnificent Arctic city, this section will provide you with all the information you want.

**Visa and Entry Requirements**

Finland is a part of the Schengen Area, which permits visa-free entry for short visits (often up to 90 days) for citizens of numerous countries, including the United States, Canada, Australia, and the majority of EU members. However, since regulations are subject to change, it is important to confirm the precise visa requirements for your nationality well in advance of your travel.

**Validity of Passport**: Ensure that your passport is valid for at least three months after the day you want to leave the Schengen Area.

**Entry by Air:** International flights are available to Rovaniemi from several European destinations, including Helsinki, Stockholm, and London, through Rovaniemi Airport (IATA: RVN). You will go through immigration and customs upon arrival, if necessary.

**Climate and Weather**

**Arctic Climate**: The subarctic climate that Rovaniemi experiences is characterized by chilly winters and mild summers. It's crucial to have suitable clothing since the temperature might change significantly depending on the season you visit.

## Winter (November to March)

Average low temperatures range from -10°C to -20°C (14°F to -4°F), with temperatures that sometimes go far below freezing.
Snowfall is frequent, resulting in a beautiful winter wonderland.
Ideal for winter sports like snowmobiling, husky sledding, and watching the Northern Lights.

## Summer (June through August)

Summertime temperatures typically range from 15°C to 20°C (59°F to 68°F), however they may rarely be higher.
Discover the phenomena of the Midnight Sun, where the sun doesn't set at night.
Ideal for outdoor activities including kayaking, fishing, and hiking.

## Currency and Money Matters

Finland uses the Euro (€) as its official currency. Although credit and debit cards are frequently accepted in Rovaniemi, including at hotels, restaurants, and stores, it is still wise to have some cash on hand for smaller purchases.

**ATMs:** You may easily withdraw cash from ATMs located all across the city as required. To prevent possible card troubles overseas, make sure your bank or credit card issuer is informed of your trip intentions.

**Currency Exchange:** Banks, currency exchange offices, and the airport all provide currency exchange services. While exchange rates may vary, they are often competitive when utilizing ATMs to withdraw cash.

**Tipping** is encouraged but not required in Finland. In restaurants and cafés, service fees are often included in the total bill. You may round up the total or add a modest tip if the service is extraordinary.

## Culture and Language

**Official Languages:** Swedish and Finnish are both recognized as official languages in Finland. However, English is a common language in Rovaniemi, particularly in the tourist sector. With residents and service providers, English will come naturally to you.

Rovaniemi is situated in the traditional heartland of the Sami people. Even though Finnish culture predominates in the city, you may also explore and discover Sami customs, art, and food while there.

## Local Customs and Etiquette

**Respect Personal Space**: Because Finns appreciate their privacy, it's important to keep your distance while speaking with them, particularly in lines and on public transit.

**Being on time** is highly regarded in Finnish society. Aim to be on time whether you are meeting a tour guide or going to a cultural event.

When entering a person's house or specific interior locations, it's usual to take **your shoes off**. Shoe racks or places intended for this purpose are often seen.

Finnish culture is deeply rooted in the use of **saunas**. It's courteous to observe the conventions, which may involve nudity bathing (separated by gender) and cool down in surrounding lakes or the snow if you've been invited to a sauna.

The traditional welcome in Finland is a hard handshake and keeping eye contact. Unless you know someone by their first name, it's traditional to address them by their last name and an honorary title (Mr. or Mrs.).

**Dining Etiquette**: Before lifting your glass at a restaurant, wait for the host to make the toast. As food waste is frowned upon, it is polite to eat everything on your plate.

Finnish people are noted for being quiet and reserved. Despite being amiable, they could come out as reserved to guests. The occasional quiet in discussions is normal.

**Respecting Nature:** Finland values its pure natural surroundings. When enjoying the outdoors, always adhere to the Leave No Trace philosophy to avoid disturbing or harming the ecosystem.

**Finally**, Rovaniemi calls with its distinct fusion of Finnish charm and Arctic enchantment. You'll be well-equipped to make the most of your visit to this interesting city by being acquainted with key travel facts, such as visa requirements, weather, currency, language, and local customs.

If you keep these things in mind, you'll be able to concentrate on the amazing adventures and experiences Rovaniemi has to offer, whether you're out searching for the Northern Lights, seeing Santa Claus, or trekking through the Arctic tundra.

## A QUICK OVERVIEW OF ROVANIEMI: The Land of the Arctic Wonders

It's important to understand Rovaniemi's distinctive character as you tour the city, which is infused with Arctic beauty, a rich history, and an alluring topography. In this part, we'll provide a high-level overview of Rovaniemi and delve into the city's unique history, geographic importance, and neighborhood structure.

**Rovaniemi's History: Echoes of the Past**

The history of Rovaniemi is a tapestry made of strands from the prehistoric Sami culture, Scandinavian influence, and the wounds of World War II. To appreciate the city's current personality, one must be aware of its past.

**Sami Roots:** For thousands of years, the native Sami people have lived in the area around

Rovaniemi. There are possibilities to learn about and engage in Sami culture and customs, which are still very important to the character of the region.

**Russian and Swedish Rule**: During the 18th century, Sweden controlled this region, which it ultimately lost to Russia. Finland didn't become an independent Grand Duchy under Russian control until 1809, which sparked further growth in the area.

**World War II:** During the Lapland War (1944–1955), in particular, Rovaniemi sustained significant damage. A large portion of the city was destroyed when the German troops withdrew. Rovaniemi was reconstructed after the war with a lot of help from other Nordic nations.

**Rovaniemi in modern times**: Rovaniemi is now the thriving capital of Finnish Lapland. In the city's architecture and museums, travelers may discover the past while making use of contemporary conveniences and services.

## Geography and Location: Arctic Heart of Lapland

Due to its strategic position, Rovaniemi serves as both a gateway to the Arctic and a prime site for seeing the marvels of the far north.

**Arctic Circle Crossing:** The closeness of Rovaniemi to the Arctic Circle is one of its most noticeable characteristics. This famous boundary is easily crossed by tourists and serves as a tactile reminder that they have crossed into the Arctic.

**Rivers and Lakes:** The city is surrounded by several lakes and is located at the junction of two important rivers, the Kemijoki and the Ounasjoki. There are many chances for outdoor recreation in this stunning natural location, including **kayaking** and **fishing**.

**Northern Lights Belt**: Rovaniemi's position inside the Northern Lights belt means that, especially during the winter months, it provides exceptional opportunities to see the captivating Aurora Borealis. Experiences with clear sky and little light pollution are improved.

Beyond the municipal boundaries, the great Arctic environment opens up, displaying magnificent woods, **icy vistas,** and **frozen rivers.** Adventurers may go snowmobiling, cross-country skiing, and snowshoeing in this environment.

**City Layout and Neighborhoods: Exploring the Urban Landscape**

The urban design of Rovaniemi displays its modernism while maintaining its ties to culture and environment. Making the most of your stay depends on your understanding of the city's neighborhoods and layout.

**City Center**: The majority of the city's eateries, stores, and tourist attractions are located in Rovaniemi's city center. Here, you may take in the local culture, see the renowned Jätkänkynttilä Bridge, and tour the Arktikum Science Center.

**Santa Claus Village** is a must-see destination for both young and elderly, and it is just a few kilometers north of the city center. The official Santa Claus post office, souvenir stores, and chances to interact with the real Santa Claus may all be found there, bringing the mythology of him to life.

**Ounasvaara** is a picturesque hill with sweeping views over Rovaniemi and the surrounding forest, located to the northwest of the city center. It is a year-round destination for outdoor pursuits, including summertime hiking and mountain biking as well as wintertime skiing and snowboarding.

**Ranta**: The Ranta area is situated along the Kemijoki River's banks and is renowned for its gorgeous riverfront views, parks, and strolls. It's a peaceful setting perfect for relaxing and taking in Rovaniemi's natural splendor.

In the western suburb of **Korkalovaara,** there are both residential neighborhoods and retail malls. It provides a window into local life outside of the busy city core.

**Jätkäsaari**: On the island of Jätkäsaari, you'll find a mixture of contemporary buildings, homes, and recreational places. It is a developing neighborhood in Rovaniemi and is well-known for its modern architecture and waterfront promenades.

**Koivusaari**: This town in the south is renowned for its parks and open spaces. It's a serene setting ideal for picnics and family activities.

**Kivitaipale**: Kivitaipale, to the east, is a mix of residential and business communities. It is a growing area of the city offering services for locals and tourists.

**In conclusion**, Rovaniemi provides an enthralling fusion of landscape, history, and urban charm. Due to its historical significance, Arctic position, and different neighborhoods, it is a multidimensional tourist destination where you can learn about Sami customs, go to the Arctic Circle, and take in the natural beauty.

You will learn about the distinctive experiences that distinguish Rovaniemi as a one-of-a-kind Arctic treasure as you explore the layout and neighborhoods of the city.

# PREPARING FOR YOUR TRIP: Ensuring a Seamless Arctic Adventure

Meticulous preparation becomes your compass as you get ready for your trip to Rovaniemi to have a successful and unforgettable Arctic experience. To assist you in making wise choices for your visit to this charming Finnish city, we'll dig into the critical elements of travel planning in this part.

**Travel Planning: Setting the Stage for Adventure**

Your trip preparation is the cornerstone of your Rovaniemi experience. With careful planning, you can make the most of your stay in this Arctic paradise. These are important things to think about:

## 1. When to Visit

The best time to visit Rovaniemi is crucial since it has a significant impact on the experiences you'll have there.

**Winter November to March**

**Northern Lights:** During the winter, Rovaniemi is well-known for its Northern Lights shows. The best time to see this natural phenomenon is during the long, dark evenings.

**Snow Adventures:** Thrilling snowmobile, husky sledding, and reindeer sleigh rides through stunning, snow-covered landscapes are all possible throughout the winter.

Santa Claus Village is a magical vacation spot for families since the Christmas spirit infuses the atmosphere there year-round.

## Summertime (June through August)

Experience the magical Midnight Sun during the summer months, when the sun never sets. It's the ideal time for golfing in the golden light, river cruises, and walks beneath the midnight sun.

**Outdoor Activities:** The lovely summer weather is perfect for outdoor activities like hiking, fishing, and kayaking.

**Sami Culture:** During the summer, there are chances to meet Sami people, participate in their customs, and eat traditional Sami food while learning about the indigenous Sami culture.

## 2. Packing Tips

For your comfort and pleasure while enjoying the many landscapes and activities in Rovaniemi, packing sensibly is essential.

## Winter necessities

**Pack insulated**, waterproof winter clothes, including thermal layers, a thick jacket, gloves, and a cap for Rovaniemi's chilly winters.

**Boots for winter:** Waterproof, insulated boots are essential for keeping your feet warm and dry while participating in outdoor activities.

**Winter Gear:** While tour companies often include thermal suits and boots for snow activities, it is advised to bring your base layers and warm clothes below.

**Camera equipment:** To capture the breathtaking Northern Lights, don't forget your camera and a tripod. In the winter, extra batteries are crucial.

## Summertime Essentials

Summers are often moderate but dress in layers still since temperatures may change quickly.

**Comfortable Shoes**: To experience Rovaniemi's natural splendor, you'll need sturdy, comfortable walking or hiking shoes.

Depending on your plans, you may want to carry **bug repellant** since the summer might bring mosquitoes and other insects.

## All Years Essentials

Finland makes use of Type C and Type F power outlets. The proper travel adapters for your electrical gadgets should be packed.

**Travel Backpack:** A dependable daypack is vital for transporting necessities on trips.

**Trip documents**: Store your passport, information about your trip insurance, and any required visas safely in a waterproof bag.

**Medication**: Make sure you have enough of any prescription drugs you use to last the length of your vacation.

## 3. Travel Insurance

Your trip to Rovaniemi must include travel insurance as a non-negotiable component. It offers assurance and financial security against unanticipated occurrences that can interfere with your goals.

**Coverage Essentials**

**Medical Coverage:** Ensure that your travel insurance has full medical coverage, which will pay for any costs associated with sickness, accident, or emergency medical evacuation.

**Choose an insurance** that covers travel cancellations or delays brought on by unforeseeable occurrences to safeguard your investment.

**Travel Delays:** In the case of weather-related interruptions, coverage for travel delays might be crucial to ensure you are compensated for extra costs spent during delays.

**Baggage & Personal Items:** Insurance may assist in defraying the expense of replacing goods if your baggage is misplaced, stolen, or destroyed.

Verify that your insurance coverage covers any adventurous activities you want to partake in, such as husky sledding or snowmobiling.

## 4. Safety and Health

Your health and safety are of utmost importance while on your Rovaniemi excursion. The following are crucial factors to remember:

### Medical Preparation

**Consult your doctor**: Before your trip, make an appointment with your doctor to talk through any travel-related immunization requirements, health precautions, and your overall health.

**Bring enough** of any prescription drugs you need, as well as copies of your prescriptions, along with you. Learn the names of your drugs under their generic names as brand names might vary from country to country.

**Travel insurance**: As was previously said, obtaining comprehensive travel insurance with medical coverage is crucial.

## Safety During Activities

**Tour Companies**: For activities like snowmobile, husky sledding, and Northern Lights excursions, choose reputed tour companies. Make sure that there are safeguards in place.

**Follow Directions**: During activities, pay close attention to the directions given by the guides. Pay close attention to safety instructions, particularly while operating a snowmobile or taking part in winter activities.

**Winter Safety**: Tell someone about your intentions and the time you anticipate returning if you're going into the Arctic wilderness. Learn about winter safety precautions including lighting a fire and calling for assistance if necessary.

**Weather Awareness**

**Stay informed**: Pay attention to weather predictions, particularly while traveling during the winter. Travel and activity plans may be affected by sudden weather changes.

**Dress Properly**: Layer your clothes throughout the winter and bring extra warm clothing, since it may be quite chilly.

**Emergency numbers:**

**Emergency Services**: Finland's emergency telephone number is 112. Keep this number on your phone and be familiar with how to dial it in an emergency.

**Embassy/Consulate**: Keep the Finnish embassy or consulate phone number handy in case you need help while traveling.

**Conclusion**: The secret to a flawless and delightful trip in Rovaniemi is meticulous planning. You'll be prepared to appreciate the Arctic marvels, colorful culture, and intriguing experiences that lie in this Finnish jewel by choosing the optimum time to go, packing wisely, getting travel insurance, and placing a priority on health and safety.

Your trip to Rovaniemi is set up to be a memorable and rewarding experience with these arrangements in place.

# ACCOMMODATION IN ROVANIEMI: Where Arctic Comfort Awaits

Choosing the ideal lodging in Rovaniemi is an essential component of your Arctic journey. Every traveler's preference may be met in Rovaniemi, whether they want the opulence of hotels and resorts, are on a budget, or are looking for unusual housing opportunities.

**Arctic luxury and Comfort Hotels and Resorts**

**Hotel Arctic Light**

Valtakatu 18, 96200 Rovaniemi is the address.

The Arctic Light Hotel is a boutique hotel in the heart of the city that provides contemporary elegance with a dash of Arctic flair. It's a favorite pick for discriminating tourists because of its stylish accommodations, excellent cuisine, and close access to Rovaniemi's attractions.

**Santa Claus Holiday Village**

Address: 96930 Rovaniemi, Tähtikuja 2.

This resort, which is in the center of Santa Claus Village, provides warm cottages, relaxing hotel rooms, and the ability to take in the all-year-round splendor of the Arctic. A variety of winter activities are available, and visitors may see Santa.

**Santasport Resorts**

Hiihtomäentie 8, 96100 Rovaniemi is the address.

Sports fans will find paradise at this resort that welcomes families. It's a terrific option for active tourists since it has cozy hotel rooms, sports facilities, a spa, and convenient access to outdoor excursions.

**Scandic Pohjanhovi**

the Koskikatu 4 in Rovaniemi, 96200
Scandic Pohjanhovi, which provides a handy central position, gives a view of the Kemijoki River. The hotel serves as a convenient home base for exploring the city thanks to its blend of contemporary conveniences and a lengthy history that dates back to 1947.

Affordable options include Arctic Comfort.

**Hostel Café Koti**

Koskikatu 9, 96200 Rovaniemi is the address.

Hostel Café Koti offers pleasant accommodations at an affordable price in the heart of the city. In addition to enjoying the on-site café, guests may choose between private rooms and dormitory beds.

**Rovaniemi Hostel**

Jorkka Järvipolku 3, 96300 Rovaniemi is the address.

Rovaniemi Hostel provides budget-friendly rooms and dorms in a tranquil location close to the Arctic Circle. It's a great option for those on a tight budget who want to take in the area's natural splendor.

**Napapiirin Saarituvat.**

Address: 4 Luostontie Street, Rovaniemi, 96930 Napapiirin Saarituvat, which is close to Santa Claus Village, provides inexpensive cottages for those looking for a peaceful getaway. For ease of self-catering, the cabins are furnished with kitchenettes.

## Unique Lodging Experience: Arctic Adventure Awaits

### Glass igloos and Arctic SnowHotel

Postal Code: 97220 Sinettä, Lehtoahontie 27, Rovaniemi
Consider staying in a glass igloo at the Arctic Snow Hotel for a unique experience. During the winter, these translucent lodgings provide unmatched views of the Northern Lights.

### Apukka Resort

Postal code: 96900 Rovaniemi, Apukka 2.
A variety of unique housing choices are available at Apukka Resort, including aurora cabins, log cabins, and wilderness tents. For those wanting an authentic Arctic experience, it's a great option.

## Resort Kakslauttanen Arctic

Kiilopääntie 9, 99830 Saariselkä is the address. Despite being a few hours distant, the famed Kakslauttanen Arctic Resort is not really in Rovaniemi. It offers classic log cabins and glass igloos for a spectacular vacation beneath the Northern Lights.

You can discover the ideal spot to call home during your Arctic adventure thanks to the range of lodging alternatives in Rovaniemi that are available to suit different spending plans and tastes. Your stay in Rovaniemi will be a highlight of your trip, whether you choose opulent hotels, affordable hostels, or unusual accommodations like glass igloos.

## GETTING AROUND ROVANIEMI: Exploring the Beauty of the Arctic

Your Arctic journey must include transportation, and Rovaniemi has a range of alternatives from public transit to vehicle rentals to fit your requirements. A tour of the city and its breathtaking environs is provided below.

**Options for transportation**

**Using Public Transit**

**City Bus**: The city and its surrounding areas are serviced by a dependable public bus system in Rovaniemi. Bus timetables are online and the routes are well signposted. Tickets may be bought online, on the bus, or via a mobile app.

**Santa Claus Express:** The Santa Claus Express is a tourism-oriented bus that transports visitors to popular destinations including Santa Claus Village and SantaPark during the peak tourist season.

**Taxis**:

In Rovaniemi, taxis are widely accessible and a practical means of transportation. You may either reserve a cab in advance or hail one on the street. Verify the taxi's license and meter status.

**Car Rentals**

Travelers who want the freedom to explore Rovaniemi and the nearby environment at their speed may consider renting a vehicle. Both the airport and the city core of Rovaniemi are home to large automobile rental agencies.

**Bicycles**

The city of Rovaniemi is bike-friendly, with designated lanes and rental options. A fun and ecological way to view the sites is by cycling across the city.

**Using Public Transit**

The effective public transportation system in Rovaniemi makes it easy to go throughout the city and its surrounding areas. What you need to know is as follows:

I) **City Buses:** Rovaniemen Liikenne Oy runs the town's local bus system. Buses are dependable, spotless, and run on time. Route plans and schedules are available at bus stations and online at Rovaniemen Liikenne.

II) When boarding the bus, you may buy tickets from the driver. While some buses only take card payments or smartphone applications, others only accept cash. There are single tickets, day passes, and annual passes available.

III) **Bus Stops**: The route number and schedule are prominently displayed at bus stops. Look for the "Rovaniemen Liikenne" sign in blue and white.

IV) **Santa Claus Express** is a dedicated bus service that links the city's core with well-known tourist destinations including Santa Claus Village and SantaPark. It runs throughout the busiest travel period.

V) **Transportation to and from the airport**: The distance between the city center and Rovaniemi Airport is around 10 kilometers. Taxis, airport shuttles, and rental cars are all options for getting to the city from the airport.

**Driving Tips and Car Rentals**

You may go at your own pace while in Rovaniemi and the Arctic tundra if you rent a vehicle. Following are some vital pointers regarding car rentals and driving in Rovaniemi:

I) **Car rental**: Rented vehicles are available from well-known agencies including Avis, Hertz, and Europcar. It's a good idea to reserve your rental well in advance, particularly during the busiest travel period.

II) **Driving Permit**: You may drive in Finland with either a legitimate national or international driving permit. Make sure you have the required paperwork, such as your rental agreement and insurance information.

III) **Winter Driving:** Be prepared for ice and snowy driving conditions if you want to visit Rovaniemi during the winter. Rent a car with winter tires, and for even more safety, think about getting an all-wheel drive vehicle.

IV) **Speed restrictions**: Become familiar with the speed restrictions in Finland. The speed limit is normally 50 km/h in urban areas and 100 km/h on highways. To avoid penalties, always obey the posted speed limits.

V) **Safety gear**: It is required to have warning triangles and luminous vests in the vehicle. Carry an ice scraper and a shovel in the winter to handle snow and ice.

VI) **Wildlife Awareness**: Reindeer, in particular, are prone to straying into highways. Be alert for them. Particularly in rural regions, go at a slower pace and be careful.

VII) **Parking**: The city core of Rovaniemi offers parking lots and garages. Make sure you abide by parking rules and pay any necessary costs.

VIII) **Fuel**: Rovaniemi has easy access to both gasoline and diesel. Major credit cards are often accepted at petrol stations, but it's a good idea to have some cash on hand.

IX) **GPS** is a useful tool for navigating the Arctic landscape. Since cellular connection could be spotty in rural regions, download your maps and navigation applications in advance.

X) **Emergency Services**: Finland's emergency number in case of an emergency is 112. Be ready by having a fundamental knowledge of Finnish traffic laws and road signs.

XI) **Using public transit**, taxis, bicycles, or rental automobiles to get about Rovaniemi and its charming surroundings is a wonderful experience. You may easily discover the city's treasures and go off on Arctic adventures by selecting the form of transportation that best meets your needs and making appropriate plans.

ROVANIEMI TRAVEL GUIDE 2023

# EXPLORING ROVANIEMI: A Journey through Arctic Wonders

Rovaniemi, the capital of Finnish Lapland, offers a treasure trove of Arctic adventures and cultural delights. In this section, we'll delve into the city's top attractions, from the magical Santa Claus Village to the educational Arktikum Science Center, ensuring your visit is a memorable exploration of Arctic beauty and culture.

**Santa Claus Village: A Year-Round Winter Wonderland**

Location: Tähtikuja 2, 96930 Rovaniemi

**Description**: Santa Claus Village is a magical place where Christmas cheer fills the air year-round. Nestled on the Arctic Circle, it's not only a must-visit for families but also a destination that allows everyone to relive the enchantment of childhood.

**Key attractions include**

**Santa's Office**: Meet Santa Claus himself, take photos, and share your Christmas wishes. He's there every day of the year.

**Santa's Main Post Office**: Send postcards and letters from Santa's official post office with a special Arctic Circle postmark.

**Arctic Circle Line:** Cross the Arctic Circle line and receive a certificate to commemorate the experience.

**Arctic Circle Husky Park:** Enjoy husky rides through the snowy forests and learn about these incredible Arctic dogs.

**Snowman World**: A winter-themed park with snow slides, ice sculptures, and an ice bar.

**Tips**: Arrive early to avoid crowds, and consider staying for the enchanting Northern Lights if visiting during the evening.

### Arctic Wildlife Park: Encounter Northern Fauna in a Natural Habitat

Location: Maa- ja metsätalousmuseo Arktikum, Pohjoisranta 4, 96200 Rovaniemi

**Description**: The Arctic Wildlife Park, located at Arktikum Science Center, allows visitors to get up close and personal with Finland's native Arctic animals. It's a place of education and conservation, where you can observe the region's wildlife in a natural setting. Key features include:

**Animal Enclosures**: See reindeer, moose, and other Arctic animals in spacious enclosures designed to mimic their natural habitats.

**Educational Exhibits**: Learn about the biology, ecology, and behavior of Arctic animals through interactive exhibits.

**Guided Tours**: Guided tours provide in-depth insights into the park's mission and the creatures that call it home.

**Photography Opportunities**: Capture stunning photos of reindeer, Arctic foxes, and more in their native surroundings.

**Tips**: Plan your visit in advance, as the park's hours and availability may vary depending on the season.

## Rovaniemi Art Museum: A Window into Northern Creativity

Location: Jätkänkynttiläntie 3, 96300 Rovaniemi

**Description**: The Rovaniemi Art Museum, also known as Korundi House of Culture, is a hub for visual arts in Lapland. This contemporary museum showcases the creative talents of local and international artists, with a special focus on northern themes. Key highlights include:

**Exhibitions**: Rotating exhibitions feature a wide range of artistic styles and mediums, from paintings and sculptures to photography and video art.

**Cultural Events**: The museum hosts cultural events, workshops, and performances, making it a vibrant hub for artistic expression.

**Korundi Café & Shop**: Enjoy a cup of coffee or browse for unique souvenirs in the museum's café and shop.

**Architectural Marvel**: The museum's striking architectural design itself is a work of art, making it an attraction worth visiting for its aesthetics alone.

**Tips**: Check the museum's website for information on current exhibitions and events to align your visit with your artistic interests.

### Arktikum Science Center: Unveiling Arctic Wonders and Culture

Location: Pohjoisranta 4, 96200 Rovaniemi

**Description**: Arktikum Science Center is a world-class institution dedicated to Arctic knowledge and culture. It's a place where science, art, and cultural heritage converge to illuminate the

Arctic's past, present, and future. Key elements include:

**Arctic Exhibitions:** Explore interactive exhibitions that delve into the Arctic's natural environment, history, and indigenous cultures.

**Northern Lights Theater:** Experience the magic of the Northern Lights in a captivating multimedia show.

**Siida Café:** Savor local dishes and flavors while enjoying picturesque views of the Kemijoki River.

**Museum Shop:** Discover unique Arctic-themed souvenirs and gifts at the museum shop.

**Tips:** Take your time to explore the museum's exhibitions, as there's a wealth of information to absorb.

**Additional Notable Attractions:**

While the above attractions are among the city's top highlights, Rovaniemi offers many more points of interest to explore:

I) **Lumberjack's Candle Bridge**: This iconic bridge over the Kemijoki River is especially enchanting when lit up during winter evenings.

II) **Lordi's Square**: Named after the Finnish hard rock band Lordi, this square is a lively gathering place with sculptures and events.

III) **Ranua Wildlife Park**: Located about 80 kilometers south of Rovaniemi, this wildlife park features Arctic and Nordic animals in a natural environment.

IV) **Korundi House of Culture**: Apart from the art museum, Korundi is home to the Lapland

Chamber Orchestra, offering musical performances and events.

Rovaniemi's attractions showcase the city's unique blend of Arctic beauty, cultural heritage, and modernity. Whether you're meeting Santa Claus, encountering Arctic wildlife, exploring contemporary art, or delving into the science of the North, each experience adds a layer to the tapestry of your Arctic adventure. Be sure to plan your visit to these attractions to make the most of your time in this captivating Finnish Lapland city.

## OUTDOOR ADVENTURES IN ROVANIEMI: Embrace Arctic Thrills

Rovaniemi, nestled in the heart of Finnish Lapland, offers a gateway to the pristine Arctic wilderness. Outdoor adventures here are more than activities; they are immersive experiences that connect you with nature, culture, and the Arctic spirit. In this section, we'll explore some of the most thrilling outdoor adventures you can embark upon in Rovaniemi, including **Husky Safaris**, **Reindeer Sledding**, **Northern Lights Tours**, and **Ice Fishing.**

**Husky Safaris: An Arctic Journey with Furry Companions**

**Location**: Various husky farms around Rovaniemi

**Description**: Husky safaris in Rovaniemi are a quintessential Arctic experience, allowing you to

harness the energy and enthusiasm of these remarkable dogs for an unforgettable adventure.
**Here's what to expect:**

**Meeting the Huskies**: Your adventure begins with meeting the huskies at a local husky farm. These friendly and energetic dogs are excited to take you on a journey through the Arctic wilderness.

**Sled Ride:** You'll be paired with your own team of huskies and a guide. The guide will teach you the basics of mushing (driving a sled), and then you'll embark on a thrilling ride through snowy forests and across frozen lakes.

**Scenic Beauty:** The landscapes you'll traverse are nothing short of breathtaking, with snow-covered trees, serene lakes, and the potential to spot wildlife. Be sure to have your camera ready for this picturesque journey.

**Duration**: Husky safaris can vary in duration, from short rides of a few kilometers to full-day adventures. You can choose the experience that suits your preferences and time constraints.

**Warm-Up Break:** Many husky safaris include a warm-up break by an open fire, where you can enjoy hot beverages and snacks while basking in the Arctic tranquility.

**Tips**: Dress warmly in layers, as temperatures can drop significantly in the Arctic. Don't forget to thank your husky team for their hard work and affectionate companionship.

### Reindeer Sledding: A Gentle Arctic Tradition

**Location**: Various reindeer farms around Rovaniemi

**Description**: Reindeer sledding is a serene and culturally rich Arctic experience that connects you with the indigenous Sami culture and the iconic reindeer. Here's what you can anticipate:

**Meeting the Reindeer**: Begin your journey by visiting a local reindeer farm, where you'll be introduced to these gentle creatures. Learn about their significance in Sami culture and their role in Arctic life.

**Sledding Adventure:** After a warm introduction to the reindeer, you'll embark on a leisurely reindeer sledding adventure. Each sleigh accommodates a couple of passengers, and you can sit back and enjoy the tranquil ride.

**Scenic Route:** Your ride will take you through snowy landscapes, with opportunities to appreciate the beauty of the Arctic wilderness. Your guide will share insights about the environment and Sami traditions along the way.

**Reindeer Herding**: Some experiences offer the chance to participate in reindeer herding activities, gaining a deeper understanding of the traditional Sami way of life.

**Duration**: Reindeer sledding experiences typically range from short rides to longer excursions, allowing you to choose the duration that suits your interests.

**Cultural Elements**: Many reindeer farms provide insights into Sami culture, including storytelling, handicraft demonstrations, and tasting traditional Sami cuisine.

**Tips**: Dress warmly and be prepared to immerse yourself in the tranquility of the Arctic wilderness.

Be respectful of the animals and the cultural significance of the experience.

**Northern Lights Tours: Chasing Aurora Borealis**

**Location**: Various locations in and around Rovaniemi

**Description**: Witnessing the Northern Lights, or Aurora Borealis, is a dream for many, and Rovaniemi offers prime viewing opportunities due to its location within the Northern Lights belt. Here's what you need to know about Northern Lights tours:

**Aurora Hunting**: Northern Lights tours are designed to maximize your chances of witnessing this mesmerizing natural phenomenon. Experienced guides lead you to the best viewing spots, which are chosen based on weather conditions and aurora forecasts.

**Prime Locations**: Rovaniemi's surrounding wilderness, with its minimal light pollution, provides an ideal backdrop for Northern Lights displays. Popular locations include frozen lakes, forests, and open fields.

**Timing**: The Northern Lights are visible during the winter months when nights are longest and skies are darkest. Tours are typically conducted in the evening and can last for several hours.

**Photography Tips**: If you're a photography enthusiast, some tours provide photography guidance and equipment to capture the Northern Lights in all their glory.

**Warmth and Comfort**: Northern Lights tours often include a break around a campfire, where you can warm up with hot beverages and snacks while waiting for the auroras to dance across the sky.

**Tips**: Dress warmly in multiple layers, as you'll be spending time outdoors in sub-zero temperatures. Bring your camera and tripod for capturing the magical moments.

### Ice Fishing: A Traditional Arctic Pursuit

**Location**: Frozen lakes and rivers in the Rovaniemi region

**Description**: Ice fishing is not just a pastime; it's a cherished part of Arctic culture, offering a unique opportunity to connect with nature and indulge in a tranquil activity. Here's what you can expect:

**Ice Fishing Basics:** Your guide will provide you with the necessary equipment, including ice fishing rods and augers to drill holes in the ice. You'll receive instructions on how to ice fish effectively.

**Frozen Landscapes**: You'll head out to a frozen lake or river, where you'll drill holes through the thick ice to access the frigid waters below. The pristine surroundings and silence of the Arctic winter make for a serene experience.

**Patience and Perseverance**: Ice fishing requires patience, as you wait for fish to bite. While you wait, take in the beauty of the frozen landscape and perhaps even spot local wildlife.

**Catch and Cook:** If you're lucky, you may catch Arctic char, perch, or other local fish species. Some experiences include preparing your catch over an open fire, savoring the fresh flavors of the Arctic.

**Duration**: Ice fishing excursions can vary in length, from a few hours to a full day, allowing you to choose the duration that suits your interests.

**Tips**: Dress warmly in layers, as you'll be outdoors in the cold for an extended period. Embrace the opportunity to disconnect from the modern world and immerse yourself in the Arctic wilderness.

**In conclusion**, Rovaniemi's outdoor adventures are an invitation to embrace the Arctic's natural beauty, indigenous cultures, and the thrill of Arctic activities. Whether you're mushing with huskies, gliding through snowy forests with reindeer, chasing the Northern Lights, or engaging in the serene art of ice fishing, each experience reveals a unique facet of Rovaniemi's charm. As you embark on these adventures, you'll create lasting memories and forge a deep connection with the Arctic wonderland that is Rovaniemi.

## EXPERIENCING FINNISH CULTURE: A Gastronomic Journey Through Finnish Cuisine

Finnish food is one of the most delectable ways to get fully immersed in this country. Discovering Finnish culture is a multifaceted experience. The tastes and customs of Finnish cuisine provide a wonderful and genuine window into the history of the nation. We'll dig into must-try Finnish foods, dining manners, and the exciting world of regional food markets in this part.

**Must Try Dishes: Enjoying Finnish Delights**

The natural resources of the nation and the cyclical nature of the seasons have a significant impact on Finnish cuisine, which combines rustic simplicity with distinctive tastes. Here are some foods you really must eat if you want to experience Finnish culture via food:

a) **Karjalanpiirakka (Karelian Pasties):** These delicate, oval-shaped pastries have a rye crust and are often filled with rice porridge, mashed potatoes, or a filling of carrots and rice. They often come with egg butter on top.

b) **Kalakukko**: A traditional fish pie from Finland, Kalakukko is cooked with pork and fish—typically perch or salmon—and covered in a rye crust. It is a filling meal that is linked to the Savonian area.

c) **Lohikeitto (Salmon Soup)** is a well-known Finnish comfort meal, particularly in the chilly winter months. It is a creamy salmon soup with a dill taste that is often served with rye bread.

d) **Ruisleipä (Rye Bread):** A mainstay of Finnish cuisine, rye bread is renowned for its thick texture and robust taste. Cold meats, cheese, and butter are often served with it.

e) **Green pea soup** known as hernekeitto is typically served on Thursdays. It often comes with a side of ham, mustard, and a warm pancake for dessert.

f) **Poronkäristys (Sautéed Reindeer)** is a Lappish dish made from thinly sliced reindeer meat that has been sautéed with onion and butter. It often comes with lingonberry sauce and mashed potatoes.

g) **Kaalikääryleet (Cabbage Rolls):** Sauteed cabbage leaves loaded with a combination of rice, spices, and ground beef.

h) **Karjalanpaisti** is a hearty stew from Finland prepared with beef, lamb, pig, and root vegetables that is cooked gently in the oven until it is aromatic and soft.

i) **Salmiakki**: A delectable specialty from Finland, salmiakki is a salty licorice candy that takes some getting used to. Locals often appreciate it as a candy or ice cream flavor.

j) A sweet and light dish cooked with lingonberries or other berries, sugar, and semolina is called a **vispipuuro**. It often has milk or cream on top.

**Dining Etiquette: Embracing Finnish Table Manners**

Understanding and following Finnish dining etiquette is a crucial component of the cultural experience while eating in Finland:

**Being on time** is important since it is respected highly in Finnish society.

Table etiquette is quite casual in Finland. Avoid putting your elbows down while keeping your hands on the table.

**Maintain eye contact** with the person you are toasting while lifting the glass. Before taking a drink, it's usual to exclaim "**Kippis!**" (Cheers).

**Wait for the Host**: If you're a visitor in a Finnish house, you should hold off on eating until the host starts the meal.

Even while eating pizza or hamburgers, **use utensils** to devour your meal. It's seen as polite.

**Tipping**: Tipping is expected although not as generously as in some other nations. It is usual in Finland. Although it's customary for service costs to be included in the bill, a 10% gratuity is always appreciated.

A simple "**Kiitos ruuasta**" (Thank you for the food) is a polite way to express gratitude to the host for the dinner.

**Shoes Off Inside:** To keep the inside of Finnish houses clean, it is traditional to take off your shoes before entering, particularly in the winter.

**Local Food Markets: A Culinary Adventure**
Consider visiting regional food markets to experience Finnish cuisine and culture at their fullest. Like many Finnish towns, Rovaniemi features bustling markets where you may taste regional specialties and interact with the locals:

The hub of Rovaniemi's culinary culture is the market in the city's center, known as **Rovaniemen Kauppatori**. Fresh fruit, berries, mushrooms, seafood, and regional handicrafts are all available here. It's a great area to sample authentically Finnish foods from food carts, such as salmon soup and Karelian pasties.

**Ounasvaara Farmers' Market**: This temporary market provides a range of regional goods against the picturesque Ounasvaara fall. Fresh berries, mushrooms, and handcrafted products may all be purchased there.

Watch for regional cuisine festivals and events, like the **Arctic Market**, where you may try delicacies like smoked salmon, reindeer meals, and berry products straight from regional farmers.

Using Finnish food as a way to learn about the culture is a voyage of tastes and customs. Each culinary experience in Finland deepens your awareness of this unique country.

Whether you're enjoying a bowl of salmon soup in a warm restaurant, learning to prepare traditional Finnish recipes, or delighting in regional delicacies at a market. The tales, customs, and shared experiences that make up Finnish cuisine are just as important as the food itself in creating a memorable cultural experience at every meal.

# Embracing the Finnish Sauna Tradition & Spa Retreats: Saunas and Wellness in Finland

Saunas are an integral part of Finnish culture and well-being; they are more than simply a place to unwind. The country's spas and health facilities provide a variety of restorative experiences, and Finnish saunas are known internationally for their distinctive traditions. Let's explore the Finnish sauna culture and the havens of tranquility offered by spas and wellness facilities.

**A Cultural Gem: The Finnish Sauna Tradition**

The term "**sauna**" alone brings up ideas of relaxation, steam, and wood. Saunas are an essential component of everyday living, social interaction, and general well-being in Finland. Here is a more detailed explanation of the Finnish sauna custom:

Sauna etiquette states that you should take off your clothes and cover yourself with a towel before entering a Finnish sauna. Finns take sauna etiquette seriously, stressing respect for personal space and privacy. Nudity is prevalent but not required.

**Löyly**: Löyly is the steam produced when water is poured over a hot sauna burner. It's a ceremonial act and the experience of löyly changes based on the sauna's humidity and temperature. Some people enjoy their löyly steaming hot, while others like it more chilled.

**Bathing** in a sauna involves repeated cycles of warmth, perspiration, cooling, and relaxation. It's common to cool down by leaping into a neighboring lake or rolling in the snow during the winter after a heated session in the sauna.

**Whipping**: Birch or juniper branches are often found in saunas and may be used to gently whisk the skin. This is said to promote relaxation and improve circulation.

**Year-round Sauna Use:** Even in the dead of winter, taking a sauna is a common ritual among Finns. The Northern Lights or frozen lakes provide for some of the most remarkable sauna experiences.

**Sauna in the Wilderness**: Finland is home to a wide range of saunas, from classic wood-fired saunas to saunas on boats or in isolated wilderness lodges. The experience is made more exciting by exploring these saunas.

**Spa and Wellness Centres: Retreats of Relaxation**

While saunas are a fundamental component of Finnish culture, spas and health facilities elevate the relaxing experience. For those seeking pampering and refreshment, Rovaniemi offers a variety of spa and wellness options:

**Arctic Spa**: The Arctic Spa, which is a part of Santa Claus Holiday Village, provides a variety of services such as massages, facials, and body wraps. Additionally, you may relax in their hot tubs and saunas while taking in views of the Arctic Circle.

**The Rantasipi Pohjanhovi Hotel** Spa is a conveniently placed spa that provides a range of health treatments, including facials and massages. After a day of Arctic exploration, its saunas and pool provide a peaceful setting to relax.

About an hour from Rovaniemi, the **Revontuli Resort & Wilderness** Spa provides a genuine Arctic escape. In a purely natural location, their wilderness spa offers saunas, outdoor hot tubs, and relaxation spaces.

**SantaSport Health & Spa Hotel**: This kid-friendly health center has a spa, exercise rooms, and a variety of activities. They include saunas and Jacuzzis where you may unwind after a day of swimming or exercising.

**Local Wellness Facilities**: Rovaniemi is home to several regional wellness facilities that include massages, aesthetic services, and relaxation techniques. These facilities often use regional herbs and organic products, as well as Arctic components, in their therapies.

Consider sessions at a woodland wellness center for a distinctive wellness experience. These escorted excursions take you into the tranquil Arctic wilderness where you may spend time in nature and benefit from its healing properties.

## Tips for Sauna and Wellness Experiences

Reservations are sometimes required at spa and wellness facilities, so making reservations in advance is a smart idea, particularly during the tourist season.

**Cultural Sensitivity:** Be considerate of regional traditions and etiquette while going to public saunas. Always be considerate of others' privacy and interests.

**Dress code**: You don't need to bring your towels or bathrobes since most saunas and wellness facilities have them available. For saunas where clothes are required, you may wish to bring swimwear.

**Stay hydrated** by sipping on water or herbal teas to replace any lost fluids, particularly while using saunas.

**Local Treatments**: To improve your overall well-being, think about experimenting with treatments that include regional ingredients, such as Arctic herbs or organic items.

The Finnish sauna tradition and spa culture combine at Rovaniemi to provide a unique experience of relaxation and cultural immersion. You will feel revitalized and incredibly connected to the Finnish way of life after partaking in any of these activities, whether you decide to have a relaxing massage, join a woodland health trek, or bask in the heat of a traditional sauna.

# FESTIVALS AND EVENTS:
## Celebrating the Spirit of Rovaniemi Year-Round

A lively city with a full cultural calendar, Rovaniemi captures the character of the Arctic area. There's always something spectacular going on in Rovaniemi, from customary festivals steeped in Finnish culture to one-of-a-kind occasions that highlight the majesty of the Arctic. Discover the yearly festivities and unique events that make Rovaniemi a popular destination for both residents and tourists all year long.

### Rovaniemi's Annual Celebrations: Embracing Finnish Traditions

**Lappi Week** (Lapin viikko) is a yearly event that lasts for a whole week and features Lappish customs and culture. It generally takes place in late February or early March. Festivals include musical performances, art exhibits, and other activities that reflect the distinctive history of the area.

**Midsummer** (Juhannus) is a lovely time of year in Rovaniemi and is celebrated across Finland in late June. To take part in bonfires, midnight sun, and other customary events, locals go to the countryside. The "**white nights**" give this event a magical touch.

**Rovaniemi Week:** This annual festival, which takes place the first week of September, features a wide range of activities, from athletic events and family-friendly activities to concerts and art exhibits. It's an opportunity for residents and guests to interact and recognize the lively culture of the city.

**Luminous Finland 100:** To commemorate Finland's 100th year of independence, this one-of-a-kind event was held in 2017. With the staging of several cultural and artistic events, like light installations and performances, Rovaniemi played a big part in the celebrations.

The start of the Christmas season in Rovaniemi is signaled by the formal opening of Santa Claus Village, which happens during the last weekend of November. Santa Claus' triumphant entry, joyous marketplaces, and the opportunity to take part in the Christmas enchantment are all included.

**Special Events Calendar: Year Round Highlights**

In addition to the yearly festivities, Rovaniemi conducts several unique activities all year long that bring tourists from all over the world:

**Arctic Design Week**: This design event, which takes place in February, features the top Arctic architecture, fashion, and design. It explores the interaction between design and the Arctic environment via exhibits, seminars, and talks.

**The Rovaniemi Marathon**, which takes place in July, presents a special Arctic challenge for runners. Choose from a full marathon, half marathon, or 10K run while taking in the beautiful scenery of the city and its environs.

**Northern Lights celebration (Valoa Rovaniemelle):** This celebration, which takes place in January and February, honors the Northern Lights and the splendor of winter. It has light installations, art displays, and cultural activities that make the winter evenings more cheerful.

**Arctic Comic Festival:** This yearly celebration of the comics and graphic novel industries is usually held in November. It features exhibits, seminars, and chances to interact with comic book creators from Finland and beyond.

**Simerock**: In August, Rovaniemi hosts the annual Simerock rock festival, which brings together musicians from Finland and throughout the world. It's a high point for music lovers.

Every few years, the **Rovaniemi International Air Show** showcases aircraft from all over the globe in breathtaking aerial demonstrations. Both aviation aficionados and the general public will find it to be an exciting event.

**Arctic Circle Jukola**: One of the biggest relay-orienteering competitions in the world, it draws competitors from many different nations. It's a thrilling and difficult tournament held in the Arctic tundra in June.

**Scientific Festival (Tiedekeskus Pilke):** This yearly event in May promotes scientific and environmental awareness and provides interesting activities and interactive displays for guests of all ages.

**Arctic Week at Rovaniemi**: This event, which takes place in October, emphasizes the importance of the Arctic and the difficulties it confronts. It includes talks, roundtables, and exhibits that focus on Arctic science, culture, and sustainability.

The dates and specifics of events might change from year to year, so it's best to check the official event websites or local listings for the most recent information before making travel plans to Rovaniemi.

There is plenty for everyone to enjoy throughout the year in Rovaniemi, thanks to its lively events schedule, whether you're interested in cultural festivals, outdoor activities, or creative exhibits.

## BEYOND ROVANIEMI

The Lapland area around Rovaniemi beckons with even more natural beauties and adventures waiting to be discovered, while the city itself provides a multitude of Arctic experiences and cultural pleasures. Here, we'll go outside of Rovaniemi and learn about three fantastic day trips and excursions:

**Korouoma National Park**, **Ranua Wildlife Park**, and a day excursion to the **Arctic Circle** are all recommended.

### Arctic Safari at Ranua Wildlife Park in Lapland
Location: 97700 Ranua, Ranuantie 129

### Overview of Ranua Wildlife Park

The Ranua Wildlife Park, which is roughly 80 kilometers south of Rovaniemi, provides a rare chance to see Arctic and Nordic wildlife in a tranquil, open environment. Families, animal lovers, and anybody else keen to see up close the splendor of Northern flora should take this day excursion.

## What to anticipate

**Animal Encounters:** Polar bears, reindeer, lynx, moose, and wolverines are just a few of the more than 50 species of Arctic and Northern creatures that may be seen in Ranua Wildlife Park. The park's roomy cages closely resemble the animals' native habitats and enable up-close yet secure viewing.

**Arctic Charm:** The park's calm setting, amid Lapland's natural environment, makes it the perfect location to take in the peace of the Arctic. You'll have plenty of chances to take beautiful pictures of these amazing animals.

Exhibits and guided tours are available at the park to teach visitors about the biology, ecology, and behavior of Arctic wildlife. These encounters help you comprehend the Arctic ecology.

**Chances for Photography**: Ranua Wildlife Park offers several picture chances for both amateur and professional photographers. Take pictures of the lively actions of Arctic foxes or the smoothly swimming polar bears.

**Bird Watching**: In addition to animals, the park is a wonderful location for birdwatchers since it is home to a variety of bird species. Both migratory and local birds are drawn to the park's serene waters.

**Gift stores and cafés:** Ranua Wildlife Park features gift stores where visitors may purchase distinctive mementos with Arctic themes and cafés serving a variety of regional foods and beverages.

## Tips for your Visit

The park's opening times and events may change depending on the season, so make travel plans in advance.

If you want to tour the park on foot, dress comfortably in sturdy footwear and weather-appropriate clothes.
For the most recent details on guided tours and animal feeding schedules, see the park's website.

## Discovering Arctic Canyons and Frozen Waterfalls in Korouoma National Park

Location: 5 Korouomantie, Posio, 97770

### Overview of Korouoma National Park

Located around 200 kilometers north of Rovaniemi, Korouoma National Park is a secret treasure of Arctic scenery. For hikers and environment lovers, this day excursion offers stunning vistas of frozen waterfalls, rocky valleys, and unspoiled wilderness, making it a must-visit location.

## What to anticipate

**Canyon marvels**: Korouoma National Park is renowned for its imposing canyons, some of which have cliffs that reach a height of 100 meters. In the winter, the ice creations on the cliffs are very beautiful.

Several magnificent frozen waterfalls, including the **Ahvenkoski** and **Jyrävä** waterfalls, can be seen in the park. These cascades become ice sculptures in the winter, giving the area a fantastical feel.

**Hiking paths:** The park has a network of well-defined hiking paths that range in difficulty from short strolls to longer hikes. The most well-known climb leads to breathtaking vistas with views of ice waterfalls and valleys.

**Cross-Country Skiing**: In the winter, cross-country skiers find Korouoma National Park to be a refuge, with groomed paths providing a special chance to glide through the pure Arctic environment.

**Photography Paradise**: Korouoma's natural beauty offers many options for taking beautiful pictures, whether you're a beginner or a seasoned photographer. Particularly spectacular periods for photography are sunrise and sunset.

**Aurora Hunting**: If you go during the long, dark winter, the park's isolation and low levels of light pollution make it a great place to take pictures of the Northern Lights.

## Tips for your Visit

Wear layers of clothes to be warm, and depending on the season, don't forget to pack strong hiking boots or winter gear.
Before setting out on a walk or ski vacation, check the trail conditions and the weather prediction.
If you don't already possess the necessary outdoor gear, you might think about renting it before visiting Korouoma National Park.

## Crossing the Magical Line on a Day Trip to the Arctic Circle

Location: 96930 Rovaniemi, Santa Claus Village

## Overview of a day trip to the Arctic Circle

The Arctic Circle is a must-see destination, and Rovaniemi provides the only chance to cross the enchanted boundary where the Arctic Circle starts.

You may take part in Arctic customs and earn a certificate for crossing the Arctic Circle on a day excursion from Rovaniemi's city center, which is just a short drive away.

**What to anticipate**

**Arctic Circle Ceremony**: At Santa Claus Village, you may take part in a unique ceremony marking the crossing of the Arctic Circle. The awarding of a certificate as evidence of your entry into the Arctic is often part of this entertaining and meaningful ceremony.

**Meet Santa Claus**: Santa Claus Village is open all year long and offers the opportunity to do so. In the cheerful old man's official office, you may chat with him about your goals and take pictures with him.

**Arctic Shopping**: Browse Santa Claus Village's distinctive stores and boutiques for items ranging from traditional Finnish handicrafts to mementos with Arctic themes.

**Arctic Circle Line**: A marker marking the precise position of this famous circle may be found at the Arctic Circle line. It's a fantastic chance to record this important event on camera.

**Arctic Activities**: Depending on the time of year, you may be able to partake in Arctic activities like husky sledding, snowmobiling, or dining at a restaurant with an Arctic theme.

**Tips For Your Visit**

Bring your camera or smartphone to the Arctic Circle marker so you may record the occasion. Check the Santa Claus Village's opening hours and activity availability before visiting since they might change with the weather.

To experience the Arctic covered in snow, think of going to Santa Claus Village in the winter.

**Beyond Rovaniemi**, these days tours and excursions provide a variety of Arctic experiences, including animal encounters, canyon exploration, and crossing the Arctic Circle.

Your trip to Rovaniemi will be more exciting because of the variety of destinations that provide different perspectives on the marvels of Lapland. These trips display the majesty of the Arctic in all its splendor, whether you're looking for unmatched natural beauty, a taste of local culture, or life-changing experiences.

# LAPLAND ADVENTURES: Snowmobiling in the Wilderness

**Location**: Various Locations in Lapland including Rovaniemi

## Overview of snowmobiling

A fascinating excursion that lets you spectacularly experience the Arctic environment is snowmobiling in Lapland. Snowmobiling gives riders of all skill levels the chance to go over icy terrain, take in the majesty of the Arctic, and take in the breathtaking scenery.

## What to anticipate

Lapland has a network of snowmobile tracks that snake through beautiful woods, frozen lakes, and snow-covered falls. Snowmobile safaris are a popular activity in Lapland. There are a variety of guided snowmobile safaris offered, ranging from family-friendly outings to more difficult treks.

**Arctic Scenery**: Snowmobiling offers a unique viewpoint of Lapland's breathtaking landscape. You'll come across huge, snow-covered plains, coniferous woods, and, if you're fortunate, the opportunity to see reindeer and ptarmigans, two species of Arctic animals.

**Snowmobiling for the Northern Lights**: For a unique experience, think about going on a snowmobile safari at night to look for the Northern Lights. You won't soon forget the experience of riding beneath the magnificent Arctic sky while looking for the rare auroras.

**Ice Fishing and Wilderness Lunch:** Some snowmobile safaris have pit breaks for ice fishing or a wilderness lunch over an open fire, where you may indulge in regional cuisine and warm up in the quaint wilderness huts **(kotas)**.

**Snowmobile Gear:** To keep you warm and safe while on your excursion, snowmobile tour companies often include thermal suits, helmets, gloves, and boots.

**Tips for your Snowmobiling Adventure**

Lapland's wintertime temperatures may be quite low, so make sure to dress warmly in layers.

To snowmobile safely, pay attention to your guide's directions and abide by all route laws and regulations.

Bring a camera so you may record the breathtaking Arctic scenery as you go.

## Cruises on Icebreakers: Getting Around the Frozen Seas

Location: Rovaniemi and Kemi (varies by operator)

**Icebreaker Cruise Overview**

Icebreaker cruises provide the chance to travel over frozen seas aboard a large icebreaker ship, making them a unique Arctic experience. These trips give you close-up contact with Arctic ice and a chance to see how powerful these amazing ships are as they chisel through the frozen water.

**What to anticipate**

**Icebreaker Experience**: The ship's passage through the heavy ice is the highlight of an icebreaker voyage. As the ship moves ahead, passengers often feel the ship vibrate and hear the ice fracture, which creates a bizarre and thrilling environment.

**Arctic Scenic Views**: From the icebreaker, you may get a bird's-eye perspective of the frozen sea and the nearby wintery surroundings. As far as the eye can see, the Arctic is a sight to see.

**Guided Tours:** Skilful tour leaders provide information on the icebreaker's activities, Arctic fauna, and the area's distinctive ecosystem. You'll discover the ship's past and how it helped preserve access to the Arctic.

**Arctic Ocean Swimming:** On certain icebreaker voyages, guests get the unique chance to brave the icy waters of the Arctic Ocean while donning a special survival suit.

**Northern Lights Cruises**: During the winter, several tour companies offer Northern Lights icebreaker cruises that let you see the auroras from the icebreaker's deck as it travels through the Arctic night.

**Tips for your Icebreaker Cruise**

Even though the ship will be heated, you should still wear warm clothing since you may want to go outdoors to thoroughly appreciate the chilly surroundings.

Follow the crew's safety guidelines at all times, particularly while engaging in activities like swimming in arctic seas.

**Sámi Culture Center Visits: Learning About Indigenous Traditions**

Location: Multiple Sámi cultural centers in Lapland

## Overview of Sámi Culture Centers

Learning about the native Sámi people and their rich cultural legacy is made possible by visiting Sámi culture centers throughout Lapland. You may engage with the real Arctic culture by learning about Sámi customs, history, art, and way of life at these institutions.

## What to anticipate

**Interactive Exhibits:** Sámi cultural centers often include multimedia presentations, interactive exhibits, and displays of traditional Sámi items that examine the past and present of the Sámi people.

The finely produced jewelry, clothes, and other handcrafted objects that symbolize the Sámi people's close relationship to nature are shown in several **Sámi art** and **Craft galleries.**

**Cultural Workshops**: A few facilities provide cultural workshops where guests may try their hand at crafting jewelry or discovering traditional storytelling while learning about traditional Sámi crafts.

**Sámi cuisine:** You could have a chance to sample some of the regional specialties, which often include products like reindeer meat, fish, and berries, and give you a delightful flavor of Sámi culinary traditions.

**Guided Tours:** Taught by trained personnel, guided tours provide in-depth insights into Sámi history, language, and culture, enhancing the educational and entertaining aspects of your stay.

**Tips for your visit to Sámi Culture Centres**
The opening times and events provided by the particular cultural center you want to visit may differ, so be sure to check.

During your visit, be respectful of Sámi culture and customs and ask questions to find out more about their way of life.

Adventures in Lapland include the exhilarating snowmobile across the Arctic, the breathtaking icebreaker excursions over the icy seas, and the chance to explore the rich cultural legacy of the native Sami people in cultural centers. These journeys provide a more profound connection to

## PRACTICAL INFORMATION: Rovaniemi's shopping

In addition to spectacular Arctic scenery and distinctive cultural experiences, Rovaniemi, the lively city of Finnish Lapland, also has a charming retail scene where you can bring a little bit of the enchantment of the Arctic home.

This tour will examine Rovaniemi's retail scene, from the city's shopping areas to souvenir stores and local crafts.

**Souvenirs and Local Crafts: Capturing the Arctic Spirit**

In Rovaniemi, souvenirs and regional crafts may be purchased, giving you the chance to carry home treasured memories of your Arctic trip. There are many attractive shops and boutiques in the city that sell a variety of handmade goods and presents with

Arctic themes. Some of the top locations to look for mementos and regional crafts are listed below:

I) **The Arktikum Shop** is a treasure trove of regional handicrafts and souvenirs with an Arctic theme, and it is a part of the Arktikum Science Center. You may discover traditional Sámi goods there, along with apparel, pottery, books, and traditional Sámi jewelry.

II) **The Science Centre Pilke's Pilke Shop** is a store with a focus on items relating to Finnish forests and the outdoors. It's a great site to discover presents like books about Finnish woods, eco-friendly goods, and wooden handicrafts.

III) **Santa Claus Village Shops**: Santa Claus Village is a shopper's paradise with a wide selection of boutiques and shops where you can buy anything from Christmas decorations and apparel to Sámi handicrafts and distinctive Arctic goods.

Send postcards from the official Santa Claus Post Office without forgetting to do so.

IV) Shops that sell real Sámi art and crafts are known as **"Sámi Duodji"** stores. Duodji is the term used to describe traditional Sámi handicrafts. Look for items made of distinctive leather, vibrant fabrics, and jewelry with exquisite designs that are a reflection of Sámi culture and workmanship.

V) **Rovaniemi Market Square** (Rovaniemen Kauppatori) is the heart of the city and a hive of activity where locals sell fresh goods, handcrafted goods, and souvenirs. It's a fantastic location for discovering unusual goods and getting a taste of the local culture.

VI) Rovaniemi is home to several art galleries that feature the creations of regional artists. It's a great location to buy unique artwork as mementos since you may browse a wide variety of art, from paintings and sculptures to modern photography and glassware.

VII) **Chocolate & delicacies:** Rovaniemi is home to many artisanal chocolate stores that provide delicious sweets and snacks. Finnish chocolate is renowned for its high quality. Look for local treats like smoked salmon and berry items as well as chocolates with Arctic themes.

**Shopping Districts: Exploring Retail Havens**

There are various retail areas in Rovaniemi, each with its distinctive personality and selection of goods. The city offers an area to fit your interests, whether you're seeking local businesses, worldwide brands, or stylish boutiques.

**Koskikatu**: You may discover a wide range of retailers on Rovaniemi's major shopping strip, Koskikatu, including apparel stores, accessory boutiques, and home goods stores. It's a busy neighborhood with cafés and restaurants, making it ideal for a relaxing walk among the shops.

The city's main shopping district, **Revontuli Shopping Center**, is home to a variety of stores, from fashion and electronics to beauty and health. It's an easy place to do all of your purchasing in one place.

**Shopping Centers**: Rovaniemi is home to several malls with a wide range of retailers, including **Sampokeskus** and **Revontuli Shopping Center**. These malls are perfect for customers looking for convenience and diversity since they often feature special events and promotions.

**The Rovaniemi Design District** is a must-visit for everyone with an interest in design and distinctive clothing. This region is well-known for its art galleries presenting modern art as well as stores promoting Finnish and international design companies.

**Sampo Park** is a retail center with Finnish and Nordic goods that is close to the Arctic Circle. It's a great location to get mementos and souvenirs with traditional Finnish designs that capture the spirit of the Arctic.

### Practical Advice for Rovaniemi Shopping

**Opening Times**: Most businesses in Rovaniemi operate during standard business hours, however, it's a good idea to double-check the exact hours of any businesses you want to visit.

**Payment**: Although Rovaniemi accepts credit and debit cards extensively, it's still a good idea to have some cash on hand, particularly if you want to purchase in neighborhood markets or more intimate stores.

**Tax-Free Shopping**: Those who are traveling from outside the EU may benefit from tax-free purchases. Before leaving, be sure you get a Tax-Free Shopping form and follow the procedures on it to get your refund.

**English** is a common language in Rovaniemi, so you shouldn't have any problem interacting with shops or getting help if you need it.

**Local and Sustainable items:** To help the community and reduce your environmental impact, think about buying locally produced and sustainable items. Look for products that were constructed using eco-friendly materials.

**Shipping**: Inquire about shipping alternatives to have your purchases delivered to your home address if you are purchasing big or delicate things. This service is provided by many stores as a convenience.

Shopping in Rovaniemi is more than just a chance to stock up on trinkets; it's also a chance to become acquainted with Finnish Lapland's culture, appreciate the inventiveness of regional craftspeople, and find a broad variety of goods that capture the distinct essence of the Arctic. Whatever you're looking for a retail experience—gifts for loved ones or treasured memories for yourself—Rovaniemi's shopping environment is sure to please.

# COMMUNICATION AND CONNECTIVITY IN ROVANIEMI

Keep in contact with loved ones, find your way about Rovaniemi, and share your Arctic experiences with the globe by staying connected while you're there. Here is a guide to utilizing local SIM cards, internet, and phone services when visiting Rovaniemi.

**Phone and Internet Services**

**Wi-Fi Hotspots**: Many hotels, eateries, cafés, and public locations in Rovaniemi provide its patrons with free Wi-Fi. This is a practical method for getting online while you're moving about the city. The majority of motels also provide Wi-Fi to their visitors.

**Cellular Data**: Rovaniemi has decent cellular coverage thanks to Finland's well-developed mobile network. Reliable 4G and 5G networks are provided by major carriers such as DNA, Elisa, and Telia. If you want to use your own SIM card, inquire about international roaming fees with your home carrier.

**Internet cafes**: If you need to use a computer and have access to the internet, you may still find a couple in Rovaniemi, even though they are less prevalent than they previously were.

**Local SIM Cards**

Buying a local SIM card might be an affordable and practical choice if you like to have a local phone number and access to mobile data while visiting Rovaniemi. What you need to know is as follows:

**Mobile carriers**: Finland has a number of them, including DNA, Elisa, and Telia. In Rovaniemi, you may locate their shops and kiosks.

**Plans**: Different prepaid and postpaid plans with varying data, call, and text limits are offered by carriers. Tourists often choose prepaid plans because they provide them flexibility and control over consumption.

**SIM Card Purchase**: Carriers, kiosks, and even some convenience shops sell local SIM cards. Ensure that your phone can accept European SIM cards and is unlocked.

**Identification**: Since acquiring a SIM card in Finland is legally required, you can be asked for identification, such as your passport.

**Top-Up**: Prepaid SIM cards may have their data or minutes increased at carrier shops, online, or through mobile applications. Easy-to-use applications are available from several carriers to manage your account and balance.

**Coverage**: Finland has good cell phone reception even in outlying locations, so you should have a steady connection during your Lapland travels.

**Data Packages:** You may choose from a variety of data packages, ranging from tiny amounts for sporadic usage to bigger plans for frequent data consumption, depending on your requirements. Make sure to look for any specialized travel deals or discounts.

**Roaming in Lapland**: If you want to go outside of Rovaniemi to more outlying districts of Lapland, be advised that cellular service may be spotty. Major tourist hubs like Rovaniemi, however, often have decent coverage.

In addition to ensuring you have a Finnish phone number for making local calls or getting crucial information while you're in Rovaniemi, using a local SIM card may save you money compared to international roaming fees. Check the terms and conditions of the plan you choose as well as any activation or top-up instructions the carrier may have supplied.

You'll be prepared to remain connected and tell your friends and family about your adventures in the Arctic once you have a native SIM card in your possession.

# ROVANIEMI TRAVEL ADVICE AND RESOURCES: Maximizing Your Arctic Adventure

Consideration must be given to several issues while planning a vacation to Rovaniemi, including setting a budget, choosing the best excursions, and locating useful websites and applications. Here is a thorough guide to help you maximize your Arctic journey while saving money and having access to helpful information.

**Money Saving Tips**

**Travel During Shoulder Seasons**: Think about going to Rovaniemi in the spring or the fall, when lodging and tour costs may be less than they are during the winter high season.

**Book Early**: When planning a vacation, book as far in advance as possible to get the greatest prices on lodging, travel, and excursions. Discounts for early booking are common among trip providers.

**Package offers**: Look for offers that include lodging, activities, and sometimes food. When compared to scheduling each component independently, this may result in cost savings.

**Ask about student and youth discounts** on excursions and attractions if you're a student or a young tourist. In Rovaniemi, certain establishments offer student discounts.

**Cook Your Meals**: Reserve lodgings with kitchens to prepare part of your meals and save money on eating out. Local markets also provide grocery shopping options.

**Utilize Public Transit**: Rovaniemi has an efficient system of public transportation. Use buses to go about the city and save money on transportation.

**Visit Free Attractions**: Take advantage of the city's free attractions, including Santa Claus Village's Arctic Circle line marker and the parks and hiking trails in Rovaniemi.

**Tax-Free Shopping:** Take advantage of Finland's tax-free shopping policy for visitors if you want to make large purchases. When making qualified purchases, don't forget to get a Tax-Free Shopping form. Then, follow the instructions on the form to get your refund at the airport.

**Agency for Travel and Tours:**

**Visit Rovaniemi**: The city's official tourist website, Visit Rovaniemi, offers information on places to stay, things to do, and events taking place there. It's a useful tool for organizing your vacation.

**Local tour operators:** Several tour companies in Rovaniemi focus on Arctic adventures. To access a variety of activities, from Northern Lights hunts to husky safaris, do your research and make reservations directly with these tour companies.

**Consult with travel providers** that focus on excursions to Lapland if you want further information. Your whole trip may be planned with their assistance, including flights, lodging, excursions, and activities.

**Visitor Information for Santa Claus Village**: If you're in Santa Claus Village, stop by the visitor center for help with tours, transportation, and local suggestions.

Useful websites and apps

**MyRovaniemi**: The MyRovaniemi app offers the most recent details on the events, things to do, dining options, and services in Rovaniemi. It is a useful tool for getting about the city.

**Website for Visit Rovaniemi**: The official Visit Rovaniemi website provides comprehensive information on the region's sights, lodging options, and activities.

**Download weather apps** to remain up to date on the local weather in Rovaniemi, particularly if you want to hunt for the Northern Lights or participate in outdoor activities.

**Google Maps:** Use Google Maps to identify particular destinations, eateries, and tourist sites as well as to navigate inside the city.

**Websites that provide Aurora predictions**: For Northern Lights predictions during your visit, visit websites like the Space Weather Prediction Center (swpc.noaa.gov) or the Aurora Service (auroraservice.eu).

**Local News Sources:** To keep up with local news and events in Rovaniemi, visit the city's news websites or think about subscribing to its social media accounts.

**Online travel discussion boards**: If you're looking for travel advice, reviews, or queries specific to Rovaniemi, check out TripAdvisor or Reddit's r/travel.

**Apps for currency conversion**: If you work with several currencies, apps for currency conversion like XE Currency may help you monitor exchange rates.

To make sure you have access to useful tools when touring Rovaniemi, remember to conduct your study, download these apps, and visit these websites before your trip.

## LANGUAGE GLOSSARY: Common Finnish Phrases for Your Trip to Rovaniemi

Rovaniemi's native tongue is Finnish, although many residents also understand and use English, particularly those who work in tourism. However, knowing a few standard Finnish words might improve your trip and demonstrate respect for the community. These words and phrases can come in handy as you move about Rovaniemi:

Hello: Hei (pronounced like "hey").

Goodbye: Näkemiin (pronounced like "nah-keh-meen")

Ole hyvä: please (pronounced like "oh-leh hew-vah").

Thank you: Kiitos (pronunciation like "kee-tohss")

Yes: Kyllä (pronounced like "kuh-lah").

No: Ei (pronounced like "ay").

Sorry / Excuse me: Anteeksi (pronounced like "ahn-tehk-see")

Paljonko tämä maksaa: How much is this? (pronounced like "pahl-yon-koh tah-mah mahk-sah?")

Where is....?: Missä on? (pronounced like: "mee-sah ohn?")

Bathroom: WC (pronounced similarly to English)

Water: Vesi (pronounced like "veh-see")

Food: Ruoka (pronounced like "roo-oh-kah")

I don't understand: En ymmärrä (pronounced like "ehn uhm-mahr-rah")

Help: Apua (pronounced like "ah-poo-ah")

Tarvitsen taksin: I need a taxi (Pronounced like "tahr-veet-sehn tahk-seen")

I'm lost: Olen eksyksissä (pronounced like "oh-lehn ehk-suhk-sis-sah")

My name is?... Nimeni on (pronounce it as "nee-meh-nee ohn")

Can you speak English: Puhutteko englantia? (pronounced like "poo-hoot-teh-koh ehng-lahn-tee-ah?")

What time is it: Mitä kello on? (pronounced like "mee-tah kehl-lo ohn?")

I'm a tourist: Olen tourist (pronounced "oh-lehn too-ree-stee")

The majority of people in Rovaniemi are used to speaking with visitors in English, so don't be afraid to use it when necessary even though these Finnish words might be quite useful. However, making an effort to speak a little Finnish may be a pleasant way to interact with the community and enhance the quality of your vacation.

# CONCLUSION: Embrace the Arctic Magic of Rovaniemi

It is abundantly obvious as we come to a close with our Rovaniemi travel guide that Rovaniemi is more than simply a place to visit; it is a portal to the marvels of the Arctic. Rovaniemi provides a distinctive fusion of natural beauty, adventure, and cultural experiences, from the charming Santa Claus Village and the breathtaking Northern Lights to the rich cultural history of the Sámi people.

Rovaniemi enchants tourists with its Arctic appeal, whether they are seeing the city's major attractions, going on exhilarating outdoor activities, or enjoying the delicacies of Finnish cuisine.

The city is a must-visit location for those looking for something genuinely special because of its rich history, breathtaking landscape, and friendly attitude.

Remember to pack for the cold, embrace local customs, and immerse yourself in the enchantment of this Arctic beauty as you prepare for your vacation to Rovaniemi. Rovaniemi guarantees an experience you'll remember for the rest of your life, whether you're visiting to see the Northern Lights dance across the sky or just to soak in the warm welcome of the North. Let Rovaniemi captivate your heart and embrace the enchantment of the Arctic.

## When Visiting Rovaniemi, There Are 14 Things You Should Never Do.

Although traveling to Rovaniemi is a magnificent experience, it's crucial to respect the environment and local customs. Here are 14 activities you should avoid when visiting this Arctic paradise:

Don't Rely Only on GPS: GPS signals might be spotty in outlying regions, so always carry a map..

Keep a safe distance from wild animals and refrain from feeding them to avoid disturbing the wildlife.

Avoid approaching huskies or reindeer. Unattended: Before engaging with these creatures, get permission first.

Don't disturb the Northern Lights by using flash photography or making excessive noise while on a Northern Lights tour.

Follow your tour guides' safety instructions, particularly while participating in sports like snowmobile and ice fishing.

Don't Forget to Ask for Permission: Request permission before photographing residents or their property.

Don't Forget to Dress Warmly: Layer your clothing since the Arctic may be quite chilly.

Don't Underestimate Sunscreen: Sunburns may still occur in winter because snow can reflect sunlight.

Don't Forget trip Insurance: Make sure your trip insurance covers activities in the Arctic.

Don't Disrupt Sámi Traditions: When participating in a Sámi cultural event, observe traditions and show respect.

Don't Rush the Experience: Give yourself enough time to take in the grandeur of the Arctic and the leisurely way of life.

Don't Break the Silence: Enjoy the peace in the Lappish woods and stay away from loud noises.

Stay on designated trails; don't trespass on frozen lakes since the ice conditions might be hazardous.

Respect Saunas: When utilizing a sauna, observe proper sauna protocol by being quiet and wearing a towel.

You can ensure a respectful and pleasurable visit to Rovaniemi while protecting its distinctive nature and culture for future generations by keeping these rules in mind.

**(HAPPY TRAVELS)**

Printed in Poland
by Amazon Fulfillment
Poland Sp. z o.o., Wrocław